VOICES FROM AROUND THE WORLD

PACIFIC ISLANDS

FIJI

Written by Dr. Tarisi Vunidilo

NORWOOD HOUSE PRESS

Norwood House Press

For more information about Norwood House Press please visit our website at www.norwoodhousepress.com or call 866-565-2900.

© 2023 Norwood House Press.

Credits

Editor: Mari Bolte
Designer: Sara Radka

Photo Credits

page 3: ©BUTENKOV ALEKSEI / Shutterstock; page 4: ©James Strachan / Getty Images; page 4: ©ChameleonsEye / Shutterstock; page 5: ©Dimitris66 / Getty Images; page 5: ©Peter Hermes Furian / Shutterstock; page 7: ©Central Press / Stringer / Getty Images; page 8: ©John Sciulli / Staff / Getty Images; page 10: ©Te Papa / Museum of New Zealand; page 11: ©ChameleonsEye / Shutterstock; page 12: ©Alfred Burton / National Library of New Zealand; page 13: ©Keystone / Stringer / Getty Images; page 14: ©Joe Benning / Shutterstock; page 15: ©Underwood & Underwood / Library of Congress; page 17: ©maloff / Shutterstock; page 19: ©Angelo Giampiccolo / Shutterstock; page 20: ©ChameleonsEye / Shutterstock; page 21: ©Express / Stringer / Getty Images; page 22: ©Worchi Zingkhai / Shutterstock; page 23: ©Douglas Miller / Stringer / Getty Images; page 24: ©wellsie82 / Getty Images; page 25: ©StanislavBeloglazov / Getty Images; page 26: ©John Sciulli / Staff / Getty Images; page 28: ©Guy Cowdry / Shutterstock; page 29: ©Pool / Getty Images; page 30: ©Klara Zamourilova / Shutterstock; page 31: ©Scott Gardiner / Stringer / Getty Images; page 32: ©sansara / Getty Images; page 33: ©Donte Tatum / Getty Images; page 33: ©WIRACHAIPHOTO / Shutterstock; page 34: ©Marco Ramerini / Shutterstock; page 35: ©Christian Peralta / flickr.com; page 36: ©NomadicImagery / Getty Images; page 38: ©Chad Robertson Media / Shutterstock; page 39: ©ChameleonsEye / Shutterstock; page 41: ©Pierre Tostee / Stringer / Getty Images; page 42: ©Nina Janesikova / Shutterstock; page 43: ©Matthias Süßen / Wikimedia; page 44: ©Don Mammoser / Shutterstock; page 45: ©cam3957 / Shutterstock

Cover: ©Matthew Micah Wright / Getty Images; ©ChameleonsEye / Shutterstock; ©Steven Giles / Shutterstock

Library of Congress Cataloging-in-Publication Data

Names: Sorovi-Vunidilo, Tarisi, 1973- author.
Title: Fiji / by Dr. Tarisi Vunidilo.
Other titles: Fiji
Description: [Chicago] : Norwood House Press, [2023] | Series: Voices around the world : Pacific islands | Includes bibliographical references and index. | Audience: Ages 8-10 | Audience: Grades 4-6 | Summary: "The islands of Fiji are full of rich history and culture. Describes the history, customs, geography, and culture of the people who live there, and provides authentic vocabulary words for an immersive experience. Includes a glossary, index, and bibliography for further reading"-- Provided by publisher.
Identifiers: LCCN 2022026189 (print) | LCCN 2022026190 (ebook) | ISBN 9781684507504 (hardcover) | ISBN 9781684048113 (paperback) | ISBN 9781684048168 (epub)
Subjects: LCSH: Fiji--Juvenile literature.
Classification: LCC DU600 .S67 2022 (print) | LCC DU600 (ebook) | DDC 996/.11--dc23/eng/20220603
LC record available at https://lccn.loc.gov/2022026189
LC ebook record available at https://lccn.loc.gov/2022026190

Hardcover ISBN: 978-1-68450-750-4
Paperback ISBN: 978-1-68404-811-3

Table of Contents

GUIDE TO FIJIAN PRONUNCIATION

B (like the *mb* in bamboo)
C (like the *th* in feather)
D (like the *nd* in land)
Dr (like the *ndr* in laundry)
G (like the *ng* in sing)
J (like the *ch* in chair)
Q (pronounced the same as 'G' in English)

Welcome to
Fiji

Bula! Ni sa bula vinaka! These are greetings in the iTaukei language. *Bula* means "life." *Ni sa bula vinaka* is the formal greeting. It means "good life to you."

iTaukei people are the **indigenous** people of Fiji. They are known for their warm hospitality and friendliness.

Indigenous people make up more than half of Fiji's population.

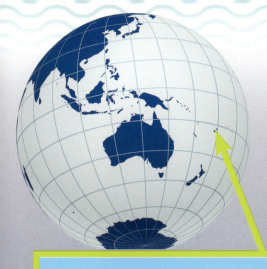

Where is Fiji?

Fiji is located in the South Pacific.
The four largest islands are Viti Levu,
Vanua Levu, Taveuni, and Kadavu.

SOUTH PACIFIC OCEAN

Vanua Levu

Taveuni

Viti Levu

KORO SEA

Suva

Kadavu

SOUTH PACIFIC OCEAN

Suva is the capital of Fiji. It is also the largest city.

CHAPTER 1
The History of Fiji

The place where the original Fijians came from is not clear. The people have stories of their ancestors sailing in a large canoe from the west. But some elders also say that Fijians did not come from anywhere—they have always been in Fiji.

The people of Fiji have close relationships with Tongans and Sāmoans. Trading and intermarriage occurred between the three islands. It is believed that the first *tabua* (whale tooth) was brought by Tongans.

Tabua is used as a form of money. It is also used in exchanges of land, as gifts of friendship, and during marriage proposals. It is passed down from one generation to another. It is important that every household keep at least one tabua to be used in special ceremonies.

There is a large tabua at the British Museum that was given as a gift by the king of Tonga to the king of Fiji in the 1800s. Other special tabua are kept at the Fiji Museum in Suva.

Tabua was given as gifts to important royal foreigners. In 1927, the grandson of Fiji's King Cakobau (right) presented tabua to Great Britain's Duke of York, later King George VI. Today, England's Royal Collection Trust holds seven tabua.

Chief Druku Lalabalavu of Tavarua Island presented tabua to Kelly Slater, a world champion surfer. Druku was one of the first Fijians who learned how to surf.

Tabua is made from the teeth of the sperm whale. Teeth were collected from whales that became beached on land. Their teeth were cleaned and polished with coconut oil. Then, they were rubbed with turmeric to darken them. A hole was drilled on each end, and a *tui ni tabua* (handle) was added. The handle is made from plaited coconut **sinnet**.

Smaller teeth were worn as jewelry. The largest tabua were used for special ceremonies such as births, weddings, baby namings, and funerals.

People on Fiji traded with Sāmoans and Tongans. Fiji's islands are full of unique items. Fiji's national bird is the collared lory. Their red feathers were used across the islands. Ironwood trees were abundant on Kabara Island. They are used for making canoes and bowls. Fiji's pottery makers were famous for their distinctive style. Today, the provinces of Rewa and Nadroga still make that style of pottery, called Lapita.

DID YOU KNOW?

Before tabua was introduced, it was believed Fijians used wooden tabua carved in the shape of a whale tooth. Shells such as conch or cowrie were also used as tabua in the past.

CHAPTER 2

Island Traditions

Fiji was first settled around 1250 BCE, or 3,000 years ago. There are many legends about the peoples' origin. What is known for sure is that the first Fiji people were part of the Lapita culture. These ancient people came from Southeast Asia. Their red ceramic pottery has been found across islands in the Pacific Ocean.

Fiji's double-hulled canoes took many skilled builders.

The first people sailed in large, double-hulled canoes called *drua*. And they brought their families. Once they reached Fiji, they raised the pigs they brought along and planted familiar food such as taro and sweet potatoes. They caught fish from the ocean. Coconut trees were harvested for food and to make furniture, cups, and tools.

Yaqona roots are pounded and water is added. Then, the drink is strained before drinking.

Homes were built from bamboo. *Bilibili* (rafts made from bamboo) let the people travel down rivers. A pepper plant known as yaqona is used to make kava, the national drink of Fiji. The plant's root is dried, pounded, and mixed with water. The drink has a peppery taste. People say they can feel their lips go numb after sipping it! During special occasions, yaqona is served in a wooden bowl and a coconut cup.

Fiji's culture has a ranking system. *Turaga* (chiefs) and *tauvanua* (commoners) are the main two. A *matanivanua* (spokesperson) speaks for the chief. *Bete* (priests) pray for the people. *Mataisau* (carpenters) build houses and canoes, and make wooden utensils. *Bati* (warriors) watch over everyone. Ranks are passed from one generation to the next.

Men traditionally dressed in a *malo* (loincloth) made from *tapa* (bark of the paper mulberry tree). Women wore a *liku* (woven skirt) woven from grass or vines. It was short and had a fringed sash. When children became adults, they were given their first malo or liku in a special ceremony. When fighting or dancing, men wore liku over their malo. Children of chiefs wore malo and liku with more designs on them.

Today, people in Fiji only wear traditional clothing during special occasions or cultural demonstrations. The fabrics have been replaced by modern materials.

Clothing, including the malo, showed a person's place in society.

Women make *salusalu* (floral garlands) as decoration during ceremonies and major life events. Colorful flowers are woven together with strips of *vau* (dried bark from wild hibiscus). Different islands have their own type of salusalu. Some flowers are only found on certain islands.

Salusalu was given to the Fijian **rugby** team after a 12-game match in England in 1970.

Fiji remained free of European contact for centuries. Famous sailors, such as Abel Tasman, Captain Cook, and William Bligh saw Fiji from a distance. But they did not stop. The islands already had a nickname—the **Cannibal** Islands.

But eventually, some braver **missionaries** arrived in 1830. They were Tahitians visiting from Tonga. Five years later, Europeans David Cargill and William Cross came to spread the gospel. The religious men had stopped at Tonga first too.

A missionary named John Hunt learned Fijian. He preached to the people in their own language. He helped translate the Bible into Fijian. Later, his Bible was printed on the island of Viwa. There were many dialects spoken at the time. His Bible was printed in Bauan, the language spoken on Viwa. Today, many people speak Bauan.

Today, around one-third of Fijians are part of the Methodist religion.

Some believe this man, photographed in 1906, to be one of the last cannibals of Fiji. But nobody knows for sure.

The Cannibal Islands

For 3,000 years, Fiji was known as the Cannibal Islands. This is because the people practiced cannibalism. Sacrifices were part of religious ceremonies. They were also made during wartime. Special wooden forks were used. Today, Fijians don't hide their history—they celebrate it. **Artifacts**, stories, and photos at the Fiji Museum educate people about the past.

Levuka was a trading post and whaling port as early as the 1820s. By 1870, it was the most important stop on the islands.

In the mid-1850s, Tonga and Great Britain began fighting over who would control Fiji's land and religion. Missionaries witnessed the wars. They wrote down what they saw.

The tribal wars ended in 1874, when Fiji became a colony of Great Britain. On October 10, chiefs met in Nasova, on the island of Ovalau. They signed a paper called the Deed of **Cession**. Ratu Epenisa Seru Cakobau was named the first king of Fiji.

New connections were not always good for the people of the island, though. In 1875, some chiefs traveled to Australia. When they returned, they carried measles with them. It spread quickly, and around one-fifth, or 50,000, of Fijians died.

People from India were brought to Fiji in 1879. They planted sugarcane. Sugar was a very important crop for England. People from the Solomon Islands and indigenous Ni-Vanuatu were also brought in. They planted and tended cotton. Levuka, the first capital of Fiji, grew quickly. Other people began spreading across the **island chain**.

DID YOU KNOW?

There are over 332 islands in Fiji. They were formed by volcanoes. Around 150 of them are inhabited. The country is divided into three state-like confederacies. They are known as Kubuna, Burebasaga, and Tovata. Fiji is further divided into 14 provinces.

CHAPTER 3

Fiji's Culture

The people of Fiji are friendly and helpful. Working together is a big part of the culture. This can be building homes, farming, or ensuring family members are healthy and cared for. Children and older people are looked after. From birth to death, Fijian families are close. They love getting together to eat, sing, and visit.

Family names are passed through generations. Traditionally, people only had one name. However, after the arrival of missionaries, people were given first, middle, and a family name. Introductions start by giving one's mother's name. Other Fijians will know where the person is from just by their name.

Passing along a name is just as important. If a person wishes a baby to be given their name, they visit the parents. They bring a woven mat and a tabua, which are presented to the parents.

DID YOU KNOW?

Fijians know how to say "sorry" if they do something wrong. It is called *soro*. Tabua is exchanged. Land disputes or fighting among friends and neighbors are a type of conflict that would result in soro.

Families in Fiji are close, and spending time with children is especially important.

Fiji's tropical environment means food is plentiful. The people eat food from the sea, rivers, and their gardens. Breadfruit, mountain apples, and lychee are seasonal and delicious fruits.

People build traditional one-room *bure* (homes). They are thatched houses made from reeds. Mataisau prepare the building materials. Then, all the men in the community come together and help build the home. Bure are warm during cold seasons and cool during hot weather. The village of Navala is made up completely of bure.

Bure can be made from anything. They are traditionally built by stacking or tying.

Despite holding onto traditions, Fiji has become Westernized too. After 96 years of British rule, Fiji became an independent nation. A ceremony was held at Albert Park in Suva on October 10, 1970. Prince Charles represented Great Britain's royal family. He read a speech on behalf of the queen. High chiefs attended too. They wore tapa, and everyone drank kava together. Ratu Sir Kamisese Mara became the first prime minister.

By this time, Fiji was full of people of different cultures. People from India, China, and England had made their homes there. Pacific Islanders from Tonga, Sāmoa, Kiribati, and Tuvalu had come too. But the country was not yet fully united. Political takeovers in 1987, 2000, and 2006 disrupted the government. No blood was shed, but these conflicts affected the whole country.

Great Britain's Prince Charles first visited Fiji in 1970. He returned several times after.

Fiji's fresh food is sold at local markets, enjoyed by people across the islands, and celebrated at festivals.

Celebrations in Fiji are as diverse as the people. The Hibiscus Festival takes place in the capital city of Suva every August. First thrown in 1956, it is a weeklong celebration to commemorate the country's diversity.

Food stalls, cultural events, concerts, and a merry-go-round are only part of the fun. There is also a Pacific pageant. Women can showcase community projects. They use the event to raise money for the projects they care about. The winner goes on to represent Fiji at the Miss Pacific Islands Pageant later in the year.

The Sevu ceremony is held in churches. It usually takes place in February. The people use this time to celebrate the good things in their life. They also ask for a good harvest in the future. People wear their best clothes and join in prayer. Crops, like taro, yam, and fruit, are placed in baskets. The baskets are laid out at the front of the church. At the end of Sevu, the food is given to those in need.

Ratu Sir Lala Sukuna Day takes place on April 22. It remembers the death of Ratu Sukuna, a chief and soldier. He protected the land and the iTaukei people.

Ratu Sir Lala Sukuna studied in England, fought with France during World War I (1914–1918), and served the people of Fiji.

There are also cultural events brought to Fiji by **immigrants**. The New Year is celebrated on January 1. Big parties are held in the streets of Suva and Nadi. Because Fiji is so close to the international date line, it is one of the first countries to end the old year and greet the new.

Chinese New Year is celebrated in February. China and Fiji have worked together for nearly 50 years. Fijians of Chinese descent celebrate their success. They look ahead to the future. Art performances and food stalls share Chinese culture with everyone.

Lion and dragon dances are part of Chinese New Year celebrations.

A large part of Fiji's population is of Indian descent. Diwali is a national holiday. Even non-Hindu people join in on the fun. This festival is a time for giving thanks and prayer. It takes place in October or November. Greetings, gifts, and notes of love remind people they are part of a community. School children learn about Diwali in school too. Themed assignments, singing, and art projects teach them the importance of this holiday.

Hindus celebrate Diwali for five days. Diwali is also known as the Festival of Lights.

Children learn ceremonies and customs from their parents.

Baby showers are a special time for new families. People visit the new baby. Mats made from pandanus plants and tapa are exchanged. Some are heirlooms. Others are made just for the occasion. Laying mats during any celebration is an act still done by women. The mats create a sacred space for ceremonies. Young girls learn proper technique from their mother or aunts.

During one special ceremony, children are taken to their mother's village for the first time. They are given tabua. This is a way to help children meet their ancestors. It also helps them connect to the land.

When a man asks for the hand of a woman in marriage, tabua is exchanged. The woman is asked three times if she accepts the man's request.

The bride and groom wear *masi* (bark cloth) during a wedding. Masi is still made on Vatulele in Nadroga province and on Moce Island. After the wedding, another tabua ceremony is held. This reminds the husband to look after his new wife.

When someone passes away, tabua is presented to the mother's family. Funerals are a remembrance of life. People wear bright colors to honor the person who is gone.

CHAPTER 4

Fiji Today

Many people from different cultures call Fiji home. Nearly 60 percent of them are iTaukei. Indians make up the next largest group, at nearly 40 percent. Indigenous people called Rotumans make up 1.2 percent. These people live on Rotuman Island and small surrounding islands in northern Fiji. The rest are people of European and Pacific Island descent.

Indigenous Fijians have been officially known as iTaukei since 2010.

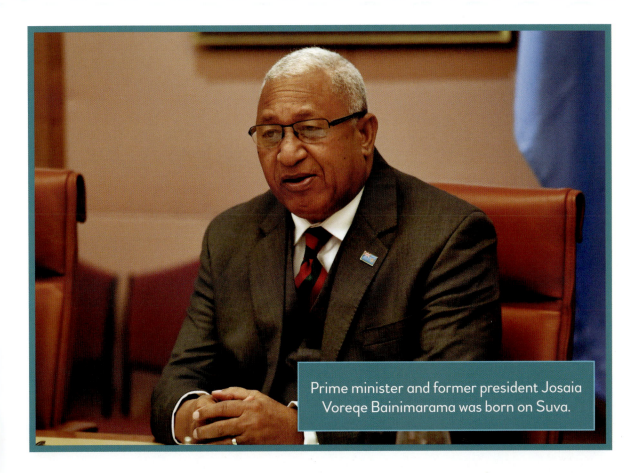

Prime minister and former president Josaia Voreqe Bainimarama was born on Suva.

The chief system is still in place. A prime minister and president take care of larger issues that face the country. The current government came into power in 2006. They are working hard to make Fiji more modern and independent.

There are three national languages spoken—English, Fijian, and **Hindustani**. There are also 300 dialects spoken across the islands. Schools are mainly taught in English, but Fijian is spoken too. There are also Chinese schools. Hindustani is becoming a more popular language for students.

Students may have to travel long distances to go to school. Some catch rides on trucks or buses. Others must walk, or even ride a boat. Children from outer islands leave home on Sunday afternoons. They attend boarding school for the week. Then, they head home on Fridays.

Public school is free for everyone.

There are both public and private schools. Most private school students are children of **expatriates**. Uniforms are picked by schools. Collared shirts, skirts, shorts, and pants are typical. Each school selects its colors.

Kids in Fiji love sports. Most children learn how to swim as soon as they can walk. Annual sports events pit schools against each other. They are divided into primary school and secondary school categories. First, school teams compete in matches against their classmates. The winners go on to regional tournaments by zone. The top-tier players compete in a national competition. Some even go on to international meets. They play against nearby countries like New Zealand and Australia. From primary school players to the highest level, Fiji's love of rugby puts the country on the world stage. Playing professionally for the Drua is the dream of many young fans.

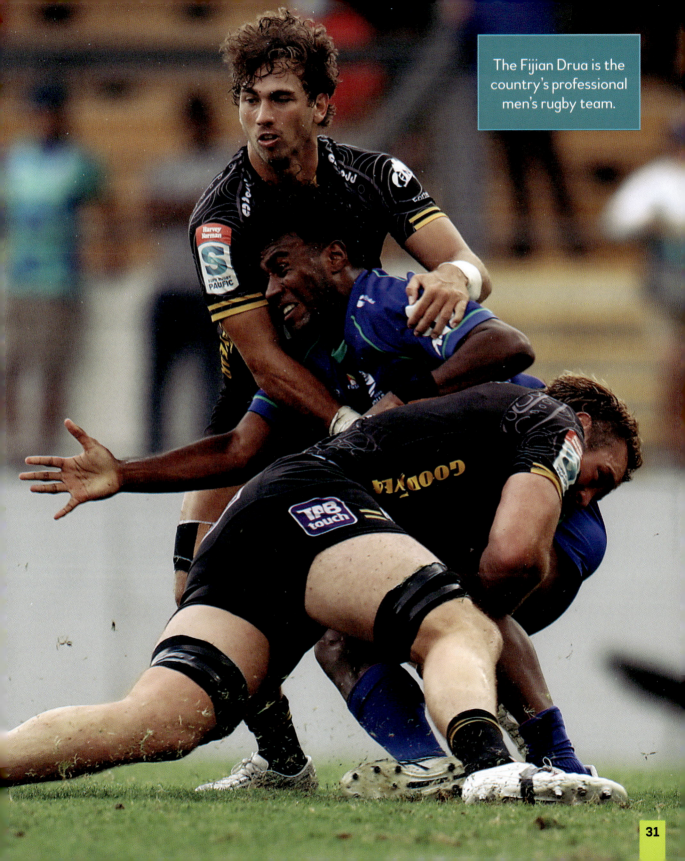

The Fijian Drua is the country's professional men's rugby team.

Pineapple is a growing industry in Fiji.

Around 45 percent of islanders still live in rural areas. There are about 1,200 iTaukei villages scattered across the islands. The iTaukei people plant gardens on land passed down for generations. They grow enough food for their families. Root crops, fruit, vegetables, and livestock are common. Some farmers also grow things like cocoa, ginger, coffee, and vanilla to sell for extra money.

Recently, the idea of returning to the land has become popular. City people can reconnect with family by growing food together.

Fiji's volcanic soil is rich and full of **nutrients**. Taro is the most important and common crop. Finding new places to grow taro has led to **deforestation** across the islands. The government has been working with farmers. They want to find more sustainable and chemical-free ways to grow it.

Volcanoes create islands, enrich soil, and help cool the planet.

What Is Taro?

Taro is a starchy root vegetable native to Southeast Asia. It has a slightly sweet and nutty flavor. The outside is brown, and the inside is white flecked with purple. It can be cooked like a potato. Both the leaf and the root can be eaten. People enjoy taro every day and on special occasions.

Fiji is full of customs and traditions. Some, like chiefs and tabua, still exist today. Other traditions are becoming less common. In fact, some customs and traditions have been completely left behind.

One example is *veiqia* (tattooing). For centuries, young women were tattooed at puberty. It was a female-only art form. It was done in secret caves by *daubati* (tattoo artists). The place that would be covered by a woman's liku was tattooed. Some tattoo symbols showed a person's **status**.

Kava ceremonies are still done in villages across Fiji.

Veiqia was banned in the 1800s. Missionaries frowned on it. They saw it as a link to ancestral worship. Over time, knowledge of the tattoos was lost.

The Veiqia Project

A group of Fijian women in New Zealand and Australia are working to revive the knowledge of veiqia. Gallery exhibitions have brought veiqia art and information to the public. Modern veiqia artists take inspiration from 19th-century drawings. They re-create them or add their own twists.

Fijians do not hide their ancestors' pasts. Instead, they embrace and learn from them.

Cannibalism is another custom that has been left behind. This practice died out around the same time as veiqia. Reverend Thomas Baker was the last missionary killed and eaten in 1867. Legend says he took a comb from a chief's hair, a huge offense. The remains of his shoes can be seen at the Fiji Museum. In 2003, the descendants of Baker's killers apologized to the man's descendants.

Bilibili could carry people and produce from the highlands.

In the past, Fijians participated in *yavirau* (fish dives). Vines were collected, braided, and turned into rope. Then, the people would load it onto boats and head out to sea. The rope was let out into the water, and people swam next to it to hold it in place. Then, the rope was slowly hauled back in. The people would use palm fronds to scare the fish trapped inside the roped-in area. The fish were pulled into shallow water and killed. Everyone in the village got a share of the fish.

Today, yavirau is not a common practice. It requires many people. Special occasions or visitors are instances where fish dives are planned.

Bilibili were once used by people in the highlands. They would use them to travel down rivers to get from the mountains to the sea. A long pole was used to push it along. In modern times, trucks or buses have replaced the rafts. They are mainly built so tourists can see them.

The double-hulled canoes that brought the first people to the island are rare today. Very few people know how to make them. The Uto ni Yalo Trust and the iVolasiga Vou are two voyaging projects. They hope to rebuild interest in sailing canoes.

Today, people can use regular handheld radios or download a Fiji radio app onto their smartphones.

Modern technology has changed everyday life. In 1935, the Fiji Broadcasting Commission was formed. It brought radio broadcast across the islands. Stations broadcast programs in English, Fijian, and Hindustani.

Communicating by radio was—and continues to be—the most popular way to communicate. Radio telephones send voice signals over radio waves. Police cars, ships, and airplanes all have radio telephones.

Electricity arrived in 1968. At the time, around half of the country's electricity was powered by diesel. But using renewable energy sources, like hydropower, wind power, and solar power, has become more important. Nearly one-third of all energy in Fiji is from a renewable source.

Around half the population uses the internet. Connectivity is poor or even nonexistent on some of the more remote islands. Most people in Fiji have cell phones, though. They help families communicate, even when they are far apart. In 2021, Fiji launched a 20-year national development plan that will enhance both the wired and wireless network across the country.

Cell phones in Fiji are called "mobiles."

Fiji is the ideal location for rugby fans! Playing rugby is a way for people from different villages to work together as a team. Four major rugby competitions are held in Fiji alone. Other competitions take place across the Pacific Islands and around the world. Many Fijian kids dream of playing rugby at the national or international level. Fiji holds two Olympic Gold medals in men's sevens rugby. A public holiday was declared after the Olympic team won its first medal in 2016.

Surfing is another reason people visit. The small island of Tavarua is world famous for its unique wave, created by an underwater reef. The wave that breaks over the reef is called Cloudbreak. Discovered by surfers in 1983, Tavarua has eight prime surf spots. But Cloudbreak is a challenge that calls to expert surfers. Challenging to catch and dangerous to fall from, the monster wave is fast and thrilling.

Even if you never make it to Fiji, you may have seen it on the big screen. Warm, sandy beaches and clear blue water attract filmmakers from around the world. In 2017 alone, 74 different movies were shot there. The show *Survivor* has been shot on Mamanuca Island since 2016. *Cast Away*, *Adrift*, and *The Blue Lagoon* are some of the movies shot in Fiji.

Catching a wave at Cloudbreak is something surfers around the world dream about.

The southwestern side of Viti Levu is known as the Coral Coast.

Tourism is a huge source of income for Fiji. Nearly 900,000 people visit every year. Australians and New Zealanders are the most common visitors. It's just a short three-hour flight from both countries. Americans and Europeans like to get away on the islands too.

Nadi Airport is on Viti Levu, and tourists tend to stick close to it. The Coral Coast and Mamanuca are nearby, stretching along the island's west and south edge. The Coral Coast is full of palm-lined beaches and family-friendly resorts. Snorkeling, surfing, and diving are popular activities. Mamanuca is a string of 20 islands. Visitors can reach them by ferry.

Fiji's third-largest island is Taveuni. It is part of the Vanua Levu islands in the north. It is also called the "Garden Island." Indigenous plants and animals live in the island's prehistoric rain forest. Many native birds fly among the trees.

Seeing both the outer islands and the interior cities is the only way to get the full taste of Fiji. The Fiji Museum in the capital city, Suva, holds historical objects that are 3,500 years old. Tabua, cannibal forks, pottery, and canoes are only a few of the ways tourists can appreciate Fijian culture.

The Fiji Museum also holds artifacts from across the South Pacific.

Visitors can walk to Wainibau Falls on Taveuni Island. They can admire the falls and then go for a swim.

Tourists can come and experience Fiji's culture and scenery for themselves. But one thing they can't take with them is tabua. In the past, some visitors were allowed to bring tabua home. But the iTaukei people are fighting to stop the practice. They believe that cultural values should be respected, not bought and sold.

Respectful visitors should also dress modestly. In some villages, women are just beginning to wear pants. Humbleness, politeness, and a desire to learn are tools that will serve any visitor well. Fijians are friendly and welcoming. They are happy to answer anyone who has an honest question.

Fiji is a beautiful place to live. To many Fijians, it is a place to unwind and forget the worries of life. Whether you're taking a vacation, going on an adventure, or visiting family or friends, there is much to see, learn, and do.

Some things on Fiji may change, but the importance of tabua continues.

DID YOU KNOW?

With whales becoming more endangered, the number of tabua available is shrinking. At one point, almost all families in Fiji had tabua. Tourists took tabua home with them. It was also given away to important people as gifts. Because of this, there is a much smaller supply. Today, a single tabua is very expensive.

Fijian Glossary

Remember to check page 3 for tips on pronunciation!

bati: warriors

bete: priests

bilibili: rafts made from bamboo

bula: life

bure: homes

daubati: tattoo artists

drua: double-hulled canoe

liku: woven skirt

malo: loincloth

masi: bark cloth

mataisau: carpenters

matanivanua: spokesperson

ni sa bula vinaka: good life to you

salusalu: floral garlands

soro: an apology

tabua: whale tooth

tapa: bark of the paper mulberry tree

tauvanua: commoners

tui ni tabua: handle

turaga: chiefs

vau: dried bark from the wild hibiscus plant

veiqia: tattooing

yavirau: fish dives

English Glossary

artifacts (ART-uh-fakts): objects of cultural or historic interest

cannibal (KAN-uh-buhl): a person who eats the flesh of other humans

cession (SESH-uhn): formally giving up rights, property, or territory

deforestation (dee-fohr-uh-STAY-shuhn): the act of removing an area of trees

expatriates (eks-PAY-tree-ayts): people who live outside their native country

Hindustani (HIN-doo-stan-ee): a group of languages spoken in northwestern India

immigrants (IM-uh-gruhnts): people who move to a new country

indigenous (in-DIJ-uh-nuss): native to an area

island chain (EYE-luhnd CHAYN): a line of neighboring islands

missionaries (MISH-uh-nehr-ees): people sent to promote Christianity in a foreign country

nutrients (NOO-tree-yunts): substances that provide nourishment for growth and life

rugby (RUG-bee): a team game that involves kicking, carrying, and passing a ball; sevens rugby is played with seven players on each side

sinnet (SIN-uht): braided rope

status (STAT-uss): the social value assigned to a person or thing

Read More about the Pacific Islands

Books

NgCheong-Lum, Roseline, and Debbie Nevins. *Fiji*. New York, NY: Cavendish Square, 2020.

Toumuʻa, Ruth. *Tonga*. Chicago, IL: Norwood House Press, 2023.

Websites

Country Reports: Fiji (https://www.countryreports.org/country/Fiji.htm) Learn about Fiji with interesting facts and current events.

The Fiji Museum—Virtual Museum (http://virtual.fijimuseum.org.fj/) Take a virtual visit to the Fiji Museum.

Index

About the Author

Dr. Tarisi Vunidilo has a MSc in Anthropology and a Postgraduate Diploma in Maori and Pacific Development from the University of Waikato, Hamilton, New Zealand. She also has a Postgraduate Diploma in Arts, majoring in Archaeology, Australian National University, Canberra, and a BA in Geography, History, and Sociology, University of South Pacific, Suva, Fiji.

Tarisi has published books and articles about Fijian pottery, language, and archaeology. She is currently volunteering as Secretary-General for the Pacific Islands Museums Association (PIMA). A Professional Teaching Fellow (PTF) and Lecturer at the University of Auckland, Tarisi is currently Assistant Professor in Anthropology at the University of Hawaii-Hilo. She also holds a Post Doc position with the University of Gottingen in Germany as part of the Sensitive Provenances-Human Remains from Colonial Contexts (2021–2024).

Reading 1

TRAVELS TOGETHER

Fifth Edition

bju press®

Greenville, South Carolina

READING 1: TRAVELS TOGETHER
Fifth Edition

Writers
Jennifer Olachea, MEd
Wendy Huffman, MEd

Contributing Writers
Gina P. Bradstreet
Stephanie Suhr, MEd

Writer Consultant
Katie Klipp, MEd

Biblical Worldview
Brian Collins, PhD
Bryan Smith, PhD

Academic Integrity
Jeff Heath, EdD

Instructional Design
Rebecca del Toro, MEd
Rachel Santopietro, MEd
Lisa Zaspel, MEd

Educational Technology
Jenny Copeland, EdD

Editor
Natalie Bonczek

Design Consultant
Michael Asire

Lead Designer
Brenna Short

Cover and Book Designer
Kristiana Olson

Sunny Lane Character Design
Kenneth Anderson

Cover Illustrator
Heath McPherson

Illustrators
Kenneth Anderson c/o Lemonade Illustration Agency
Alfredo Belli, Advocate-Art Inc. Collaborate Agency
Elena Bia
Lisa Fields
Gergely Fórizs (Beehive Illustration)
Marina Halak (Beehive Illustration)
Heath McPherson
Carlo Molinari, Advocate-Art Inc.
Filippo Pietrobon (Beehive Illustration)
Elena Selivanova (Beehive Illustration)
Benji Williams
Allyson Wilson

Production Designer
Jennifer Stuhl

DesignOps Coordinators
Kaitlyn Koch
Lesley Ramesh

Permissions
Maria Andersen
Sharon Belknap
Stacy Stone
Carrie Zuehlke

Project Coordinator
Abby Ray

Postproduction Liaison
Peggy Hargis

Photo credits appear on page 204.

Text acknowledgments appear on page 205, which is an extension of this copyright page.

The text for this book is set in Acme Gothic by Mark Simonson, Adobe Minion Pro, Adobe Myriad Pro, Adorn Slab Serif by Laura Worthington, ASAP by Omnibus-Type, Athelas, Avenir Next, BD Supper Bold by Lopetz, Belda by Jeremy Dooley, Calibri by Monotype, Century Gothic Pro by Monotype, Filson Pro by Olivier Gourvat, Free 3 of 9 by Matthew Welch, Grenadine MVB by Akemi Aoki, Helvetica, Henderson Slab Basic by Alejandro Paul, Highgate by Dalton Maag, Marvin by Patrick Griffin, Merriweather by Eben Sorkin, Miller Text by Matthew Carter, Mr Eaves Sans by Zuzana Licko, Report by Ray Larabie, Rogliano by Rodrigo López Fuentes, Rosella by Sabina Chipara, Sirenne Text MVB by Alan Dague-Greene, Sofia Pro by Olivier Gourvat, Sweater School by Ray Larabie, Tablet Gothic by TypeTogether, Times, Times New Roman PS, Times New Roman PSMT, Tondo by Dalton Maag, and Turnip RE by David Jonathan Ross.

Previously published as READING 1C: *Helping Hands*

© 2024 BJU Press
Greenville, South Carolina 29609
Fourth Edition © 2012, 2019 BJU Press
First Edition © 1981 BJU Press

Printed in the United States of America

ISBN 978-1-64626-440-7

15 14 13 12 11 10 9 8 7 6 5 4 3 2 1

Brave Together

CONTENTS

iv

CONTENTS

Brave Together

Who helps me to be brave?

Big Question: What does it mean to be brave?

Comparing Text and Video

How is listening to or reading a story from a book different from watching a video about the same story? How is it the same? Which do you like better?

Vocabulary Words

afraid
brave

Dragons and Giants

fantasy from *Frog and Toad Storybook Favorites*
by Arnold Lobel

Frog and Toad were reading a book together.
"The people in this book are brave," said Toad.

"They fight dragons and giants, and they
are never afraid."

"I wonder if we are brave," said Frog.
Frog and Toad looked into a mirror.
"We look brave," said Frog.
"Yes, but are we?" asked Toad.

Frog and Toad went outside.
"We can try to climb this mountain," said
Frog. "That should tell us if we are brave."
Frog went leaping over rocks, and Toad came
puffing up behind him.

They came to a dark cave.
A big snake came out of the cave.
"Hello lunch," said the snake when
he saw Frog and Toad.
He opened his wide mouth.
Frog and Toad jumped away.
Toad was shaking.
"I am not afraid!" he cried.

They climbed higher, and they
heard a loud noise.
Many large stones were rolling
down the mountain.

"It's an avalanche!" cried Toad. Frog and
Toad jumped away. Frog was trembling.
"I am not afraid!" he shouted.

They came to the top of the mountain.
The shadow of a hawk fell over them.
Frog and Toad jumped under a rock.
The hawk flew away.
"We are not afraid!" screamed Frog and
Toad at the same time.

Then they ran down the mountain very fast.

They ran past the place where
they saw the avalanche.

They ran past the place where
they saw the snake.

They ran all the way to Toad's house.

"Frog, I am glad to have a brave friend like you," said Toad.
He jumped into the bed and pulled the covers over his head.

"And I am happy to know a brave person like you, Toad," said Frog.
He jumped into the closet and shut the door.

Toad stayed in the bed, and Frog stayed in the closet.
They stayed there for a long time, just feeling very brave together.

After Reading

1. What do Frog and Toad wonder when they look in the mirror?
2. What do they decide to do to see if they are brave?
3. What things do they run away from?

Think & Discuss

Do you think Frog and Toad are brave?
Why or why not?

Big Question: How can two people be both alike and different?

Connecting Text to Self

When you read a story, think about yourself. Does the story remind you of something you have done? Do you know anyone like the characters in the story?

Vocabulary Words

everything
look
right
together

Tip Top Twins

realistic fiction by Jennifer Olachea
illustrated by Allyson Wilson

Jake and Blake are twins.
They look the same.

They have the same beds.
They have the same hats.

They like the same games.
They like the same snacks.

But not everything about them is the same.
Jake has a pet snake named Zane.
Blake has a pet cat named Buzz.

Blake likes to bake cupcakes.
Jake likes to skate by the lake.

15

Jake and Blake once traded places in class.
Jake said, "I am Blake!"
Blake said, "I am Jake!"
Miss Gale had to put tape on them to tell
the right name for the right twin.

Dad and Mom and Jake and Blake went on
a plane to see Grandma.
Jake did not like the plane. He was afraid.

Blake said, "Be brave, Jake! We can have fun!"

Together, Jake and Blake had fun on the plane.
Jake and Blake love being twins!

1. Why do Jake and Blake look the same?
2. What is different about them?
3. Why does Miss Gale put tape on Jake and Blake?

Think & Discuss

How are you like your friends?
How are you different from your friends?

Big Question: How can people who are different be friends?

Real Life and Fantasy

A fantasy story could not happen in real life. You can tell that a story is fantasy if it has things in it that could not really happen. Does this story have things that could not really happen?

Vocabulary Words

dragon
ice cream
leaves
outside
pinecones

My Dragon, Drake

fantasy by Wendy Huffman
illustrated by Marina Halak

Drake is my dragon.
He is a big green-and-purple dragon.
We like to take hikes and pick up pinecones.

Dad made a fire outside.
We tossed the pinecones in the fire.
They smelled good.

Drake likes to help with my jobs too.
Mom asked me to do a job outside.
I had to rake the leaves.

I was tired.

I was hot.

I was alone.

Drake came to help.
We raked the leaves into a big pile.
Drake and I dived in the pile!
My legs stuck out at one end.
Drake stuck out at both ends.

Then he helped me rake the leaves back up.
He helped me put them in a big black bag.
He can pick up many leaves at one time.
Our job went fast!

Mom said we did a fine job.
She gave us two dimes to get ice cream cones.

I licked mine.
Drake ate his in one bite.
It is fun to have a dragon for a friend.

1. What does the boy like to do with Drake?
2. How does Drake help?
3. How does Drake eat his ice cream?

Think & Discuss

What do you like to do with your friends?

Big Question: What makes a dragonfly funny?

Main Idea

Remember that informational text gives facts about real life. What the text is mainly about is called the main idea.

Vocabulary Words

body
dragonfly
eats
funny
lay
long

Dragonfly: A Funny Bug

informational text by Wendy Huffman

A dragonfly is a funny bug.
A dragonfly looks a little like a dragon.
A dragonfly can be green.

It can be blue.

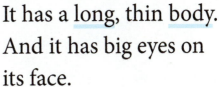

It can be orange.

It has a long, thin body.
And it has big eyes on
its face.

A dragonfly has big eyes.

A dragonfly has four wings.
It can fly in one place like a drone.

It can sit still on a thin blade
of grass or a flat stone.

A dragonfly lives by the water.

A dragonfly likes to live by a lake or a pond.

When it is time, a mother dragonfly will lay her eggs in the water.

A baby dragonfly lives in the water.

A baby dragonfly eats a lot.

It eats a lot of bugs and little fish. While it is in the water, it gets its legs and wings.

Then it must go from
the water and fly away.

Next time you are at a lake
or pond, try to spot one of
these funny bugs.

After Reading

1. What colors can a dragonfly be?
2. How many wings does a dragonfly have?
3. Where do baby dragonflies live?

Think & Discuss

What is funny about the way dragonflies look?
What is funny about what they do?

Big Question: What is a Hink Pink?

Riddles

A riddle is a tricky question with a funny answer. Usually, a riddle is a kind of joke. The riddles here are called Hink Pinks. What do you notice about that name?

Vocabulary Words

flute

yule

Rhyming Riddles

poetry by D. R. Williams
illustrated by Benji Williams

What do you call a donkey wearing a Christmas wreath?

a yule mule

What do you call a courageous boy?

brave Dave

What do you call a handsome pig?

a fine swine

33

What do you call a cloak for a purple fruit?

a grape cape

What do you call a pretty little wind instrument?

a cute flute

What do you call goo made from a green fruit?

lime slime

What do you call a
skeleton made of rocks?

stone bones

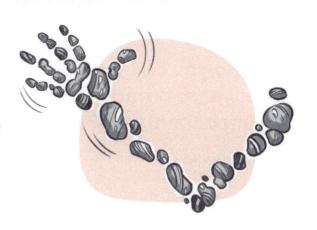

What do you call a girl
who is never on time?

late Kate

What do you call a song about
a summer month?

a June tune

What do you call the place where a small digging animal lives?

a mole hole

What do you call a very active place for bees?

a live hive

What do you call a story that is supposed to be funny but isn't funny at all?

a broke joke

1. What is special about Dave?
2. What is odd about the bones?
3. Why would a joke that is not funny be called broken?

Think & Discuss

What do you notice about each of the riddle answers?

Big Question: How can I be brave when others laugh?

  ## Characters and Setting

Remember that a character is a person or animal in a story.

The setting is where and when a story happens. Who are the characters in this story? Where and when does this story happen?

Vocabulary Words

 1

boy

first

hearing aids

played

talk

A New Friend

realistic fiction by Jennifer Olachea
illustrated by Kenneth Anderson

1 **Tim and Lucas**

Tim and Lucas played together at playtime.
They liked sliding, swinging, and running.
Tim liked to tell jokes. Lucas liked to play games.
Sometimes they played with other children.
Sometimes it was just Tim and Lucas.

A new boy came to first grade.
His name was Cole.
Cole had hearing aids to help him hear.
Mrs. Hall said, "Face Cole when you
talk so he can hear you."

At playtime, Tim and Lucas played on the swings.
Then they went to play ball with other children.
Cole was with the others.

A boy said to him, "Can you hear me? Can you say 'ball'?"
The other children laughed.

Cole's face was sad. He ran away.
Tim felt sad too.
But he did not go with Cole.
He and Lucas played ball.

Tim, Lucas, and Cole

Tim went home. He still felt sad.
He did not want his grapes for a snack.
"Why are you sad, Tim?" Dad asked.

"A new boy came," said Tim.
"He has hearing aids. The other kids
laughed at him at playtime."

43

"Did you laugh, too?" Dad asked.

"No, I did not laugh. But I did not help him," Tim said.

44

"Why not?" asked Dad.
"I was afraid they would laugh at me too," said Tim.

Dad nodded. "It is not fun when people laugh at you," he said. "You must be brave."
"What can I do to be brave?" Tim asked.

"You must ask God to help you. You must think of others," said Dad.
"Think, 'what would I want someone to do for me?'"

The next time the boys played together,
Tim went to Cole and faced him.
"Do you want to play with Lucas
and me?" Tim asked Cole.

Cole smiled. "Yes, I do!" he said.
Tim, Lucas, and Cole went to the swings.
Tim was glad God helped him to be
brave and make a friend.

1. What is different about the new boy in first grade?
2. Why is Cole sad at playtime?
3. What does Tim do that makes Cole happy?

Think & Discuss

Tell about a time someone laughed at you or your friend. How did you feel? What did you do?

The Bible says to do to others what you want them to do for you.
(Matthew 7:12)

Big Question: How can I be brave when someone I love is far away?

Soldiers

Not all soldiers go to fight. Some soldiers have other jobs, like working on airplanes, guarding buildings, or cooking food. No matter their jobs, all soldiers in a war zone could be in danger. All soldiers must be brave to do their jobs.

Vocabulary Words

1
Iraq
major
Qatar
United States

2
attack

A Brave Father

a true story by Major White with Eileen M. Berry
illustrated by Carlo Molinari

1 Major White's Trip

The United States was at war with Iraq.
Major White was packing to go
help in the war.

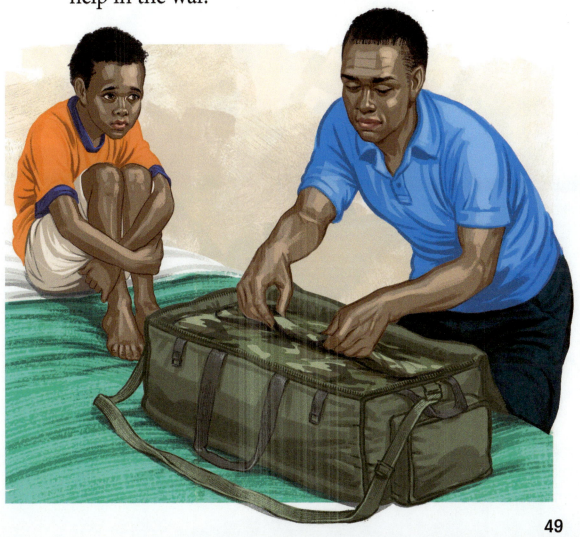

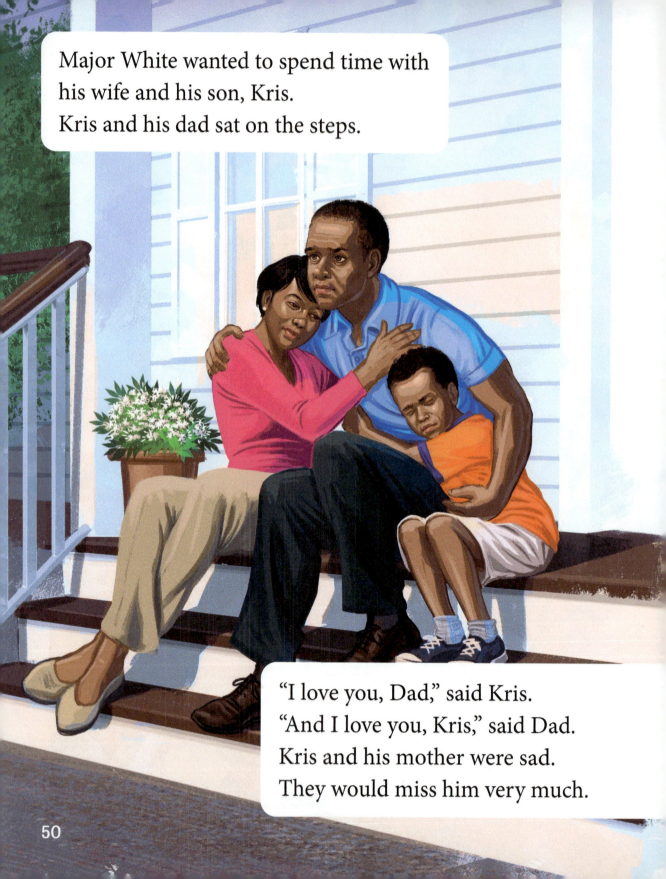

Major White wanted to spend time with his wife and his son, Kris.
Kris and his dad sat on the steps.

"I love you, Dad," said Kris.
"And I love you, Kris," said Dad.
Kris and his mother were sad.
They would miss him very much.

Major White had men who worked for him.
They had jobs to do in the war.
They would fix war planes.
Major White and his men got on a big plane.
They thought about the jobs they would do
when they got there.

At last, the plane landed at the base in Qatar.
It was time to get to work.
There were planes to fix.
Major White helped his men check the planes.

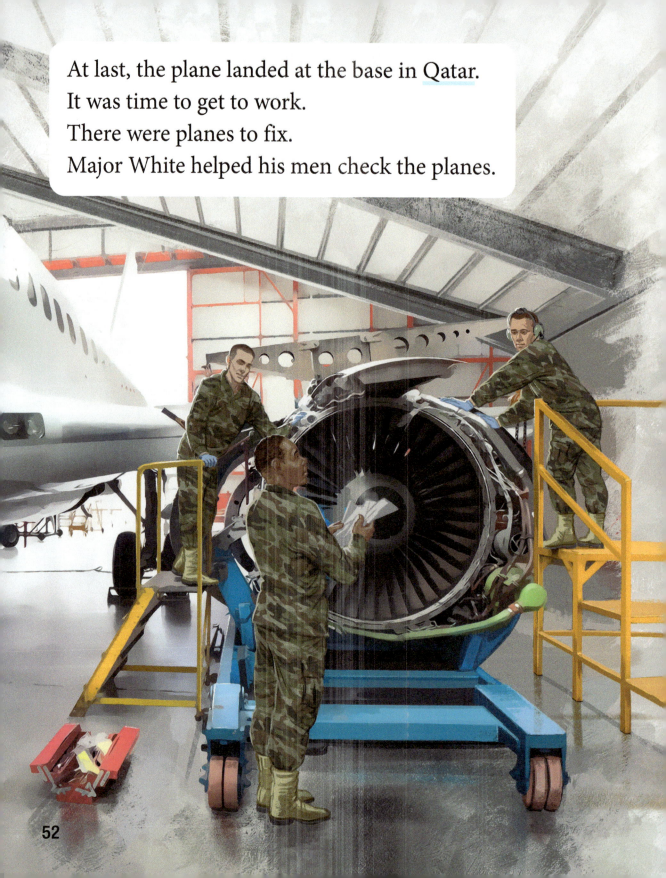

Major White missed his wife and son.
He did not like to be away from them.
But there were times to chat with them.

When Kris was waking up at home, it was past
lunchtime for his dad in Qatar.
When it was lunchtime for Kris and his mother,
it was bedtime in Qatar.

2 Glad to Get Home

It was hot in Qatar.
There was sand everywhere.
Sometimes sand got in the men's eyes.
The sand felt like little pebbles hitting
their skin.

One time, someone yelled, "Code Red!"
There could be a gas attack on the base.
What would the men do?
Major White and his men had to stop
working and put on big masks.
They waited.

But God kept them safe.
The gas attack did not come.
They were glad when it was time to
take off the masks.
The men wanted to go home where
they felt safe.

But they wanted to finish their
jobs for the United States.
They kept working.

At last, Major White said to his men,
"The job is done. It is time to make
the trip home."
They got back on the big plane.
The men were glad to go home.
The plane landed.

Mrs. White and Kris were there.
Kris could not wait to hug his dad.

"Where is Dad?" Kris asked his mother.
"Dad will come," said Mrs. White.
Then Dad got off the plane.
Kris and his mother ran to him.
They gave him a big hug.

Kris was glad that his dad had helped
the United States.
But Kris was glad to have his brave
father home.

1. Why did Major White have to leave his family?
2. What did Major White do in Qatar?
3. What did Kris do when his dad came home?

Think & Discuss

Has someone you love ever had to go far away?
How did you feel?

Big Question: How can I be brave when I am scared?

Emotions

Emotions are feelings.
Do you ever feel sad? Angry? Scared? Happy?
Excited? God made us to have all these emotions.
Read this Bible account about Daniel. How does
Daniel feel about the new rule? How do the
bad men feel when Daniel is punished? How
does the king feel when Daniel is still alive?

Vocabulary Words

1
Daniel
knees
lions
obey
window

2
breath
keep
mouths
worship

Brave Daniel and the Lions

a Bible account by Eileen M. Berry
adapted from Daniel 6
illustrated by Gergely Fórizs

1 **Praying before God**

Daniel got on his knees. It was time to pray.

Three times a day he prayed by his open window.

But this day was not like other days.

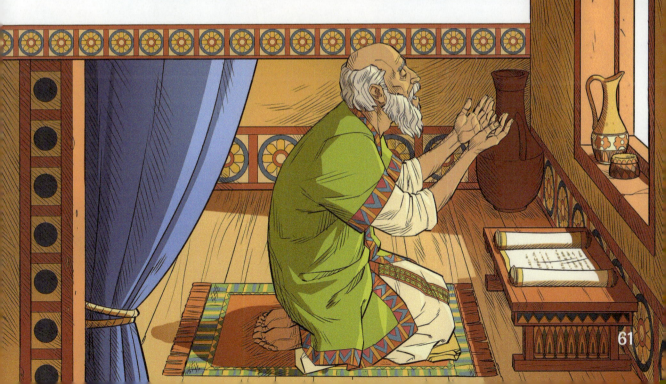

The king had made a new rule.
He said the people could only pray to the king.
Anyone who prayed to God would be put
into a den of lions.

Daniel wanted to obey God and the king.
But now, praying to God was disobeying the
king's new rule.
What would Daniel do?

"Oh, God," Daniel prayed, "I want to obey You.
I want to obey the king too.
But I must not stop praying only to You."

"Help me be brave and obey You.
I call on Your name to help me obey You."

The king's men saw Daniel on his knees.

"See?" they said. "Daniel has failed to obey
the new rule.
We must tell the king to punish Daniel."

The king was sad.
He liked Daniel.
He did not want to punish Daniel.
But the new rule must be obeyed.

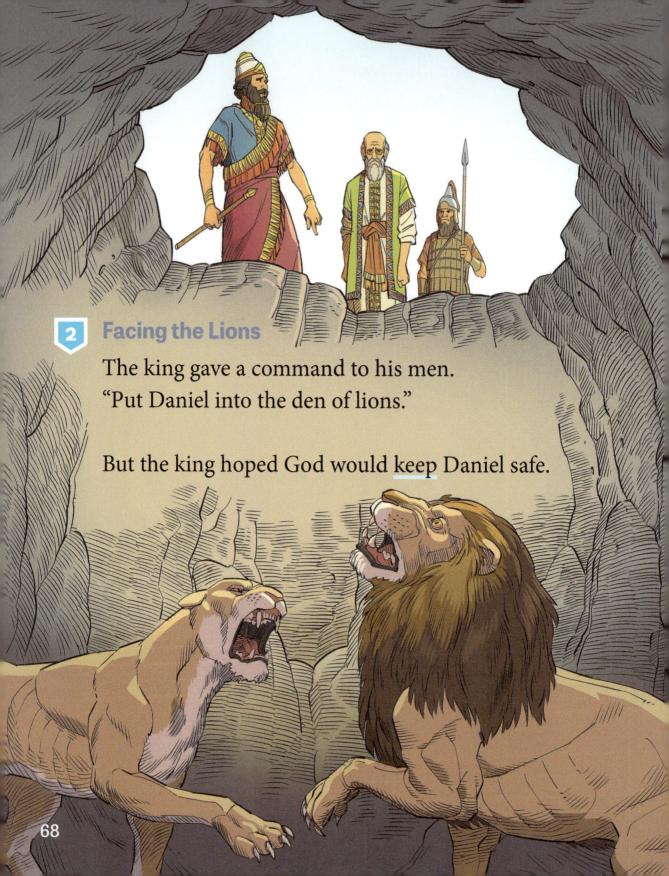

2 Facing the Lions

The king gave a command to his men.
"Put Daniel into the den of lions."

But the king hoped God would keep Daniel safe.

In the den, Daniel waited.

The lions sat.

They watched Daniel.

He felt their hot breath on his face.

He could see their tails swish.

He knew they wanted their dinner.

"Keep me safe, God," he prayed.

The lions kept their mouths shut.
Not one lion bit Daniel.

At sunrise, the king ran to the den.
"Daniel!" he yelled. "Are you safe?"

"I am fine!" said Daniel.
"My God has saved me from the lions.
He shut their mouths.
The lions have not hurt me!"

The king was glad.
He let Daniel out of the lions' den.

The king said, "God has saved Daniel from the lions!"
Then he made a new rule.
"Everyone must worship Daniel's God."

Daniel knew God had heard his prayer.
He lifted his hands in praise.
"Thank you, God," he said.
Daniel trusted God, and God made him brave.

After Reading

1. What did Daniel do three times every day?
2. What did Daniel pray to God for when the king made the new rule?
3. What did God do for Daniel because he prayed and trusted in God?

Think & Discuss

When you get scared or sad, what does God want you to do first?

What can you pray for when you feel sad or angry?

What can you pray when you feel happy or excited?

"God is my salvation; I will trust, and not be afraid."
Isaiah 12:2

? Big Question: What does it mean to be homesick?

 ## Main Character

Every story has characters. Characters can be people or animals. The main character is who the whole story is mainly about.

Vocabulary Words

1
buckskin
cabin
ranchers
sunrise
tadpoles
wade

2
began
Psalm
remind
sunset

Camp Sunrise

realistic fiction by Addy Forrest and Wendy Huffman
illustrated by Heath McPherson
character design by Kenneth Anderson

1 Homesick

It was a big day!
Dad drove Calvin and Tim to camp.
When they got there, the man at the desk
checked his list.

"Tim will be in the Blue Buckskin cabin.
Calvin, you will be in the Red Ranchers cabin."

Calvin felt afraid.
He did not want to leave his mom and dad.
And he did not want to be away for a week.
He could be brave if Tim were with him.
He wanted to be in Tim's cabin.

Calvin said to Dad, "I do not want to be in
the Red Ranchers cabin.
I want to be with my friend."

Dad said, "You must stay in the Red
Ranchers cabin.
You will like the other campers.
You will have fun.
Mom and I will come back next week to
pick you up."

Calvin did not think he would have fun.

Mr. Nick smiled at Calvin. "I'm glad you will be in the cabin with me this week. We will have fun!"

"There is a lot to do here. We will get up at sunrise. We will learn from the Bible. And we will wade in the lake and get tadpoles!"

Calvin was awake in bed. He thought and
thought. Calvin did not want to wade in
the lake. He did not want to get tadpoles.

Calvin wanted to go home. He wanted to
sleep in his bed. He wanted to play with
his friends at home.

He was homesick.

The next day Calvin got up at sunrise.
He and the other campers sat on rocks
next to the lake.
Mr. Nick read Psalm 56:3–4 from his Bible:

"What time I am afraid, I will trust in thee.
In God I will praise his word; in God I
have put my trust."

Mr. Nick said, "When we are afraid, we
must pray to God and praise Him.
He will make us brave."
Calvin prayed. Then he praised God.
Then God began to help Calvin feel brave.

Calvin had a lot of fun at camp.
He made some friends.

He rode the water slide with his
friend Dale. He went fishing with his
friends Ben and Sam. They got three fish.

He even got to sit next to Tim
by the campfire at sunset.

Calvin missed home a little less.
He prayed and trusted God.
God made him brave.

Mom and Dad came to pick Calvin up when camp ended.
Calvin gave them the craft he had made.
It was made with thin yellow sticks.

"What is this?" asked Dad.

"It is a sunrise," Calvin said with a smile.
"It will remind me of the fun I had at
Camp Sunrise.
It will remind me to pray and
trust God from sunrise to sunset."

After Reading

1. Where do Calvin and Tim go?
2. How does Calvin feel about being there?
3. What does Calvin do to help himself be brave?

Think & Discuss

Where have you been when you have
felt homesick?
What can you do when you feel homesick?

"Evening, and morning, and at noon will
I pray . . . and he shall hear my voice."
Psalm 55:17

Big Question: What do I dream of doing when I grow up?

Genre: Biography

A biography is a true story about the life of a real person.

Vocabulary Words

1
airplanes
barber
France
grew

2
America
died
flew
how
showed

Brave BESSIE

biography by Jenna Dale
illustrated by Carlo Molinari

Bessie Coleman

1 Bessie Dreams

Bessie felt the hot sun on her back. She gazed at the sky. She stuffed some cotton in her sack. "Someday I will see the world," she dreamed.

Bessie and her family picked fluffy white cotton every day. Sometimes she helped her mother wash smelly clothes for other people.

Bessie went every day to a little school.
She loved to read and write.
She was good at math.

Bessie did not like to pick cotton
or wash clothes. She dreamed of
doing something big with her life.

When she grew up, she went to live in a big city. She lived with her big brothers. She worked in a barber shop.

Bessie's brothers told her about men in the
war who could fly planes.
"I want to fly too!" Bessie said.

"You cannot fly, Bessie! Girls do not fly
airplanes," one brother said.

Bessie's other brother said, "They do in France."
Now Bessie knew she wanted to fly airplanes!

2 Bessie Flies

Bessie went to France where women could go to flying school.

Bessie learned to fly an airplane. She learned to do tricks in the air. She did what everyone told her could not be done. Bessie was brave.

When Bessie came home, everyone was glad. She was the first black woman in America to fly airplanes.

Bessie wanted to help other women. She flew her airplane and did many tricks. She spoke to people about flying. She wanted others to be brave like she was.

Bessie wanted to make a school where
anyone could learn to fly. But she never did.
She died before she could make a school.

Many people were sad that Bessie died. But people also wanted to be brave like Bessie was.

A man began a special club for people who wanted to fly. He named it for Bessie. Many men and women learned to fly just like Bessie.

The first members of the Bessie Coleman Aero Club

Bessie Coleman did something big with her life. She flew airplanes. And she showed people how to be brave.

Bessie with her airplane in 1922

After Reading

1. When Bessie was a little girl, what did she help her mom do?
2. Where did Bessie go to learn to fly airplanes?
3. How was Bessie brave?

Think & Discuss

Tell about one thing you dream of doing when you grow up.

Big Question: Who takes care of me?

Onomatopoeia

Onomatopoeia words are sound effect words.
What onomatopoeia words do you hear when
you sing "Old MacDonald"?
You can say, "The dog barks."
Or you can say, "The dog says *ruff!*"
You can say, "The horse whinnied."
Or you can say, "The horse says *neigh!*"

Vocabulary Words

milkman
Mueller
wagon

Trust *in God*

a true story retold by Karen Wilt
illustrated by Elena Bia

Plink, *plunk* went the cups on the plates.
Patty's cup was empty. Her plate was empty.
Mr. Mueller said, "Let us pray to God. We will
trust Him to feed us."

Squeak, *creak* went something in the street.
Patty got up to see.
"I see someone," Patty said.
"A man has come to visit us. It is the baker,
and he has something in his hands."

"I could not sleep," the baker said
to Mr. Mueller.
"I made these for you to eat."

"Thank God!" said Mr. Mueller.
"He gave us something to eat."
Mr. Mueller helped the baker
take the buns inside.

Patty put a bun on each plate.
But the cups were still empty.

Clink, clank went something in the street.
Patty ran to see.
A milkman was waiting on the steps.
"I cannot drive this wagon," he said.
"I need to fix it. Will you please take the milk?"

"Yes! We will be happy to take the milk," said
Mr. Mueller.
"And we thank God for this meal."

The buns were warm, and the milk was sweet.
They ate, and they drank.
Then *plink, plunk* went the cups back onto the plates.
"It is time to clean up," said Patty.
"I am glad God gives us each thing that we need."

After Reading

1. What was in Patty's cup and on her plate at the beginning of the story?
2. Who visited Mr. Mueller's house with buns and milk?
3. Why did God give Mr. Mueller and the children the buns and milk?

Think & Discuss

Who took care of the children in the story?
Who takes care of you?

The Bible tells us to cast all our worries and fears on God because God cares for and loves us.
(1 Peter 5:7)

? Big Question: Where is God when I am scared?

Comparing Text to the Bible

When you read a story or poem, especially one that talks about God or the Bible, it is good to compare what the text says to what the Bible says.

How does the poem "near" compare to Psalm 139 in your Bible?

Vocabulary Words

climb
deserts
mountain
protects

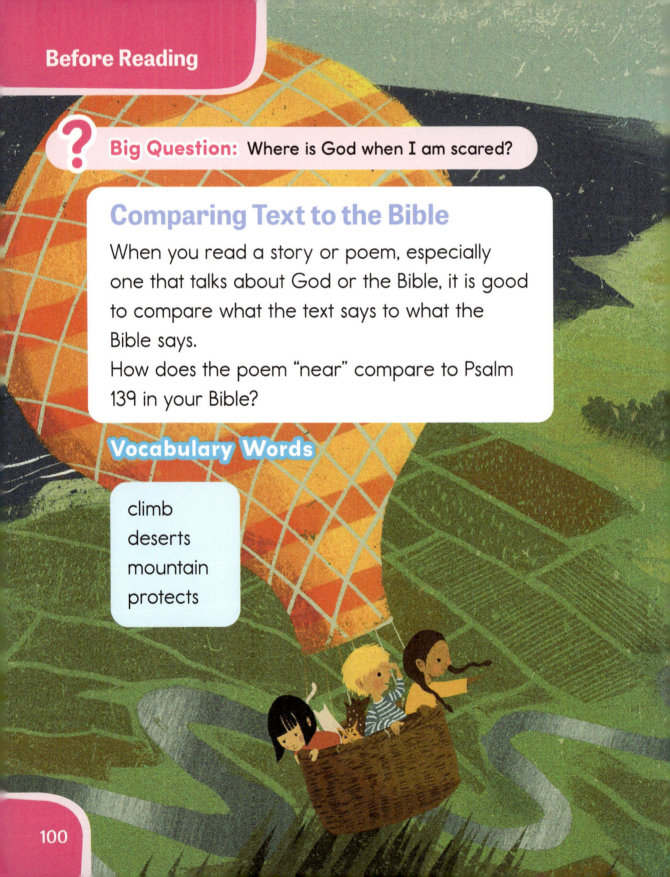

near

poetry by Sally Lloyd-Jones
based on Psalm 139
illustrated by Jago

God is my Father who made everything.
And I am a little explorer of the wide world.

He is near me
And he protects me.

He sees me
And he knows me.

He is strong
And he looks after me.

He is with me—always!

However far I go
He is always near me.

I could climb the biggest mountain . . .

I could fly to the highest star . . .

I could dive into the deepest sea . . .

I could sail far, far away—to the North Pole!

God would still be there!

I could trek through jungles . . .

ride through deserts . . .

zoom as fast as light!

God would still be there.

Even in the dark at night
He is still with me there.

He stays close to me
And he won't ever leave me.

Because I am his little child
And he loves me.

After Reading

1. Who always sees you?
2. Where will God always be?
3. Who loves you?

Think & Discuss

God is always with you. How does this make you feel when you are scared?

Big Question: How are firefighters brave?

Emergency Workers

Sometimes people have emergencies. That means people are in danger and they need special help in a hurry! Maybe a person has been hurt. Maybe there is a fire in a house. A firefighter is one type of special worker who helps people in emergencies.

What other types of emergency workers do you know about? What special way do they help people quickly?

Vocabulary Words

1
alarm
chief
down
siren
tied

2
coat
hydrant
station

Brave Firefighters

realistic fiction by Wendy Huffman
illustrated by Filippo Pietrobon

1 **Going to See the Fire Trucks**

Oliver loved fire trucks. His granddad was the fire chief.

One day, Granddad and Oliver went to see the fire trucks. Oliver could not stop smiling!

The first thing Oliver saw was a bright red fire truck.

It sat in the sun.
It sat on the driveway.

Two firemen were scrubbing it clean and rubbing it dry. It looked like a bright red candy apple.

Granddad picked Oliver up. He set him inside the cab. Oliver saw lots of buttons. He hit one. The siren made his ears hurt.

Just then, Oliver heard something much bigger.

The fire alarm rang!
Firefighters ran from everywhere!
Some slid down the silver pole.

The firefighters hopped in the long ladder truck. The ladder truck was the biggest, longest truck of all. Fireman Bob sat in the cab. He drove the truck. Fireman Jack sat high on the top. He had to steer the big long truck in the back.

"Where are they going?" asked Oliver with wide eyes.

Granddad said, "A home is on fire. A man is stuck on the top floor of his home! They must go help him. And they must put out the fire."

Fireman Bob and Fireman Jack rushed
to the fire. Granddad drove with Oliver
to the fire.

The firefighters looked at the home. They had to think fast. How will they put out the fire? How will they get the man down from the top floor of his home?

Up

Up

Fireman Jack made the ladder go Up

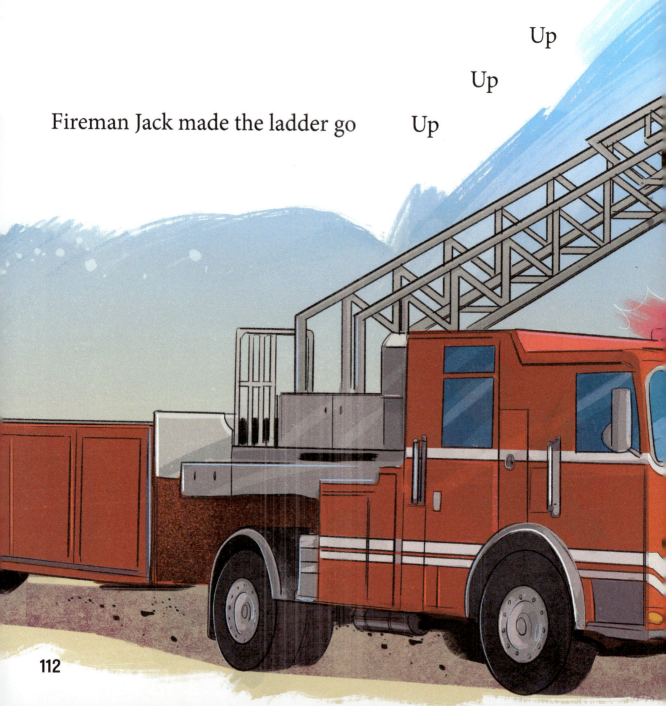

Then he tied <u>ropes</u> to his belt to be safe.

"What is Fireman Jack going to do?" asked
Oliver.
Granddad said, "He is going to go high up
the ladder to reach the man on the top floor
of the house. He will help him get down."

Putting Out the Fire

"Fireman Jack is brave," said Oliver.

"Yes, he is," said Granddad.

"Fireman Jack will use water from the fire hydrant to fight the fire."

Oliver looked at Fireman Bob. He had a funny mask on his face.

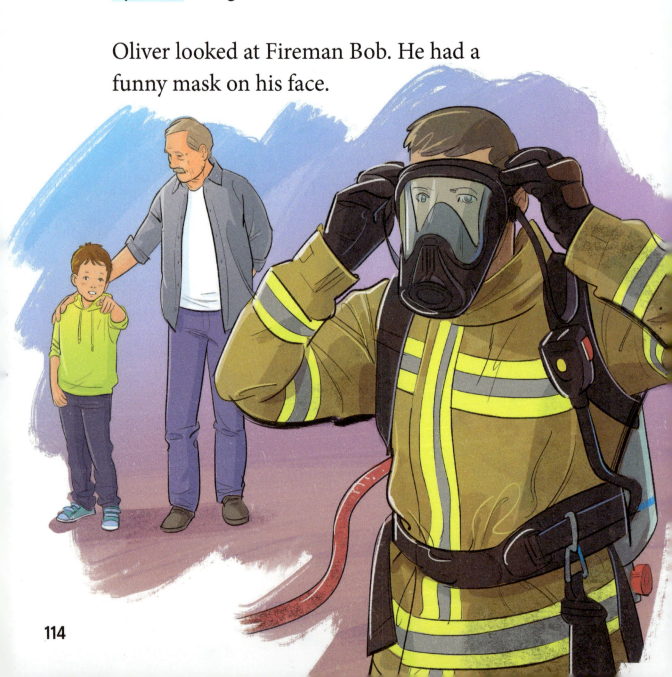

"What is that funny mask for?" asked Oliver. "The mask keeps Fireman Bob safe from the smoke. He also needs a hat and coat to keep him dry," said Granddad.

Granddad was watching his brave firefighters. He wanted to see that they had what they needed to be safe.

Fireman Bob could not get into the home.
He chopped with his ax. He cut a big hole
in the door. He needed to get inside to put
out the fire.

At last, the fire was out.
The firefighters were happy.
Oliver and Granddad clapped.

The man gripped the firefighters' hands.
He thanked them for helping him!

Oliver and Granddad drove back to the station.
Oliver thought about his day.
And Oliver was tired. He wanted to lie down.

The firefighters were tired too.

But they were not done yet.

The truck was dusty and wet. They put the fire truck on the driveway in the sun. They scrubbed and rubbed the big long fire truck.

"The fire truck looks like a bright red candy apple again!" Oliver said.

Oliver and Granddad smiled.

After Reading

1. Where are fire trucks kept?
2. What helps firefighters get people out of high places?
3. What does Fireman Bob use to get into the house?

Think & Discuss

How did Fireman Bob and Fireman Jack show bravery in the story?
How do other emergency workers show bravery?

Jesus says that the greatest love a person can have is to die for his friends. (John 15:13)

Big Question: How can an animal be brave?

Dialogue

Remember that quotation marks show when a character is speaking, as in "Hello!" said Jack. Dialogue in a story is characters talking to each other. Look for quotation marks so you can find the dialogue in a story.

Vocabulary Words

1
proper
shivered

2
scrambled
shattered

The Best Dog Yet

a true story retold by Nancy Lohr
illustrated by Elena Selivanova

1 A Stray Puppy

"Is that puppy sick, Dad?" asked Mom.
"I do not think he is sick," said Dad.
"But he is so thin. He is wet to the
skin. This stray dog needs help, Mom."

"We do not need this dog," said Mom.
Dad petted the dog. It shivered.
"You are right," Dad said. "We do not need
this dog, but he needs us. If you get a dish of
scraps, I will dry the little dog off."

Many days came and went. The puppy got
bigger and bigger. He was a fluffy, happy
dog. He ran and tumbled in the grass. He
yipped at Mom. He yapped at Dad. At night,
he slept on the rug by the bed.

One day Mom said, "This is a big dog. He needs a proper home. He needs a proper name."

"Well," said Dad, "I think he has a proper home. He can stay here. I like him, and I want him to be my dog. I will give him a name.

We will name him Rusty."

Rusty Helps

One night, Rusty smelled smoke. He whined at Dad. He licked Dad on the hand. Dad groaned, but he did not wake.

Rusty yipped at Mom. He licked her toe. "Stop, Rusty!" she said. "It is nighttime. Go back to sleep."

Rusty tugged on her sleeve.
Then Mom woke up.
"Dad! There is smoke in here!
There must be a fire!"

Dad jumped up and ran to the door.
It was hot. Dad went to the window.
It would not lift.

"Quick! The fire is getting hotter. Will we be trapped?" asked Mom.
"Not if I can lift this window. Help me," he said.

But they could not lift the window. It was shut tight.

Then Rusty pulled Mom back. He dashed for the window. Dad could not stop him. Rusty jumped up into the glass. The glass shattered, and Rusty landed on the grass below the window.

Mom and Dad scrambled after him. They
dropped onto the grass and ran from the fire.
Then they went to hug Rusty.
"Thank you, Rusty." Mom was crying. She
shivered without her coat.

Rusty groaned. He had a big cut on his back.
He was bleeding.

Dad sat next to his bleeding dog.
He patted Rusty.
"You are a brave dog, Rusty," Dad said.
"Oh, yes!" Mom said. "We will help you get well."
"You are the best dog yet!" boasted Dad.

After Reading

1. How did Rusty come to live with Mom and Dad?
2. Why did Rusty try to wake Mom and Dad up?
3. How did Mom, Dad, and Rusty escape from the fire?

Think & Discuss

Do you think Rusty was brave?
Have you ever heard of another animal being brave?

? Big Question: How do poems use rhythm?

Rhythm

Remember that rhythm is a pattern of beats or sounds. Listen to the beat of the words in these poems about snow. Can you clap to the rhythm?

SNOW

poetry by Mary Ann Hoberman
illustrated by Lisa Fields

Snow
Snow
Lots of snow
Everywhere we look and everywhere we go
Snow in the sandbox
Snow on the slide
Snow on the bicycle
Left outside
Snow on the steps
And snow on my feet
Snow on the sidewalk
Snow on the sidewalk
Snow on the sidewalk
Down the street.

A Sledding Song

poetry by Norman C. Schlichter
illustrated by Lisa Fields

Sing a song of winter,
   Of frosty clouds in air!
Sing a song of snowflakes
   Falling everywhere.

Sing a song of winter!
   Sing a song of sleds!
Sing a song of tumbling
   Over heels and heads.

Up and down a hillside
   When the moon is bright,
Sledding is a tiptop
   Wintertime delight.

After Reading

1. In the first poem, what things are covered with snow?

2. In the second poem, what are the children doing?

3. Do you think the poet likes sledding? How can you tell?

Think & Discuss

What words are repeated over and over in the poems?
Why do you think the poet did that?

"He giveth snow like wool."
Psalm 147:16

Big Question: How does my family celebrate special times?

Time-Order Words

Remember that a story sequence tells what happened first, next, and last in a story. Use words like first, next, and last to help put the story in the right order.

Vocabulary Words

1
Christmas
cookies
dough
frosting
ornaments

2
church
falling
sound
sweater

3
bowed
Joseph
Mary
sorry

A Christmas Cookie

realistic fiction by Jennifer Olachea
illustrated by Heath McPherson
character design by Kenneth Anderson

1 **Grandma's Cookies**

"Will it snow, Mom?" asked Jayla.

Mom smiled. "It may snow tonight. That would be nice," she said.

Jayla and Mom were baking together. They were making Christmas cookies. Mom rolled the dough flat, and Jayla cut the dough into shapes. They put the cookies in to bake.

137

"When the cookies are done, we will put frosting on them," said Mom. "Just like Grandma and I did when I was little."

Dad and Calvin came in. "It is time to put up the Christmas tree!" said Calvin.

Jayla clapped her hands. "May I put the candy canes on the tree?" she asked.

"Yes, you may," said Mom. "First, we will string the lights. Then we will add the ornaments. Then it will be time for the candy canes."

Calvin and Jayla helped Mom and Dad with the Christmas tree. They smelled the cookies baking.

When the tree was finished, Mom said,
"Now it is time to frost the cookies."

Calvin wanted to help too. Mom, Jayla,
and Calvin put sweet white frosting on the
cookies. The cookies were shaped like bells,
Christmas trees, and snowmen.

When all the cookies were frosted, Jayla and Calvin put red and green sprinkles on top.

"When will Grandma come?" asked Calvin.

"Grandma will come for supper tonight," Mom said. "Then we will all go to the Christmas play."

"Do you think she will like our cookies?" asked Jayla.

Mom laughed. "Yes, I think she will like them very much!" she said.

Time for Church

When Grandma came, Jayla held her hand and showed her the sparkling Christmas tree. Then Jayla showed Grandma the Christmas cookies.

"Jayla, those cookies are just like the ones your mom and I used to make!" said Grandma. "Do you think they taste just as good?"

Jayla giggled. "I know they taste good, Grandma! I ate one!"

Calvin came in with Grandma's bag. "It is snowing!" he yelled.

He and Jayla ran to peek out the window. Big white flakes were falling from the gray sky.

After supper, Jayla put on her red Christmas dress. Calvin put on his green Christmas sweater. It was time to go to the play.

When the family got to church, Calvin and Jayla watched the snow fall for a bit.

Jayla said, "What was that sound?" She and Calvin peeked under a bush.

The children saw a tiny black-and-white kitten. The little cat shivered. "Meow," it cried.

"Oh, sweet kitty!" said Jayla.

"Jayla, we should go in the church," said Calvin. He went to the church door.

Jayla picked up the kitten and put it in her coat pocket. She went inside and sat next to Calvin. She hoped the kitten would be quiet.

Calvin and Jayla sang Christmas songs. They saw some children in a play about Mary, Joseph, and baby Jesus.

They heard the preacher speak about the first Christmas. The preacher said, "Let us pray."

Jayla closed her eyes and bowed her head.
The church was quiet. Then she heard,
"Meow!"

The kitten felt warm. Now it wanted
something to eat. It jumped out of Jayla's coat
pocket and said "Meow!" again.

The preacher did not pray.
He opened his eyes and said,
"Did a cat come to church for
Christmas?"

Everybody laughed. Jayla picked
up the kitten. "*Sh*," she said.

Jayla went outside with the kitten.
Mom came too.

"Jayla, where did you get that kitten?"
asked Mom.

"I saw it under a bush," Jayla said. "He is
lost and sad. May I keep him, please?"

"We will ask your dad," said Mom.
"You should not bring cats into church."

"I am sorry, Mom," said Jayla. "The little kitty was so chilly. I thought he would be quiet."

When Dad, Grandma, and Calvin came out of the church, Dad said, "I think we can have a little cat in our home. Jayla, you got a kitten for Christmas!"

"Thank you, Dad! Thank you, Mom!" said Jayla. "I think I will name him Cookie!"

After Reading

1. What does Jayla want to show Grandma?
2. Where does the family go after supper?
3. What does Jayla find near the church?

Think & Discuss

Tell about something your family does to celebrate Christmas or another holiday.

? **Big Question:** Does my size determine how brave I am?

Genre: Fable

A fable is a made-up story that usually has animal characters who talk and act like people. A fable teaches a lesson called a moral.

Vocabulary Words

arrows
crawled
idea

The Eagle and the Ant

a fable retold by Gail Fitzgerald and Wendy Huffman
illustrated by Collaborate Agency

One hot day an ant was sitting in the sun.

"I see a stream. I will get a drink," said the ant.
But the ant slipped and fell into the blue water.

"Help! Help!" he yelled.

155

A big eagle sat in a tree close by. He saw the ant in the stream. He dropped a stick into the water.

"Grab this stick," the eagle said to the ant.

The ant bravely stepped onto the stick.

"Thank you! You saved my life," said the ant to the eagle. "Maybe someday I can help you."

The ant spent many happy days by the stream. He and the eagle became true friends.

One day two men came to the stream. The ant felt the stomping of the men's feet on the land. Up in his tree, the eagle did not feel the men's steps.

The men came to hunt. The eagle did not see the men with their bows and arrows. The ant did.

One man stopped and aimed his arrow at the eagle.

"Fly away, my friend," cried the ant with all his might.

But the eagle did not hear the ant's tiny cry. The ant had an idea. But he would need to be brave. He crawled right up to the man. He did not think about getting stepped on. He needed to help his friend.

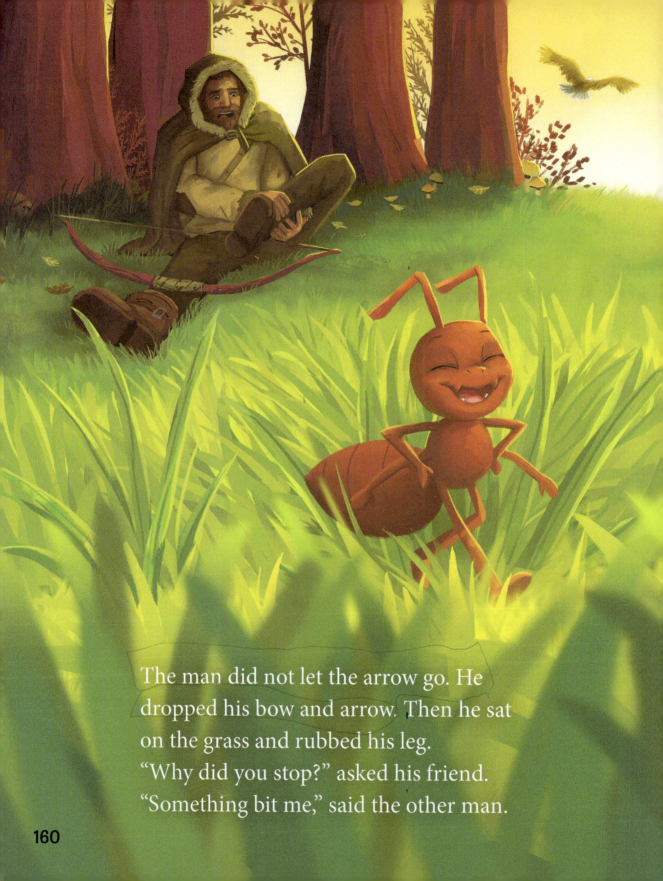

The man did not let the arrow go. He
dropped his bow and arrow. Then he sat
on the grass and rubbed his leg.
"Why did you stop?" asked his friend.
"Something bit me," said the other man.

The ant scrambled from the man's sock. The eagle flew away.

The ant went on his way with happy steps. He had been brave. He had helped when his friend was in need.

Moral: Bravery does not depend on size.

After Reading

1. How does the eagle help the ant?
2. Why is the eagle in danger?
3. How does the ant help the eagle?

Think & Discuss

Tell about a time you had to be brave.

"Be of good courage, and he shall strengthen your heart, all ye that hope in the LORD."
Psalm 31:24

Big Question: How can I be brave when I make a mistake?

Genre: Historical Fiction

Historical fiction stories tell about things that really happened, but some parts in the story are made up.

Vocabulary Words

1 President Lincoln
soldiers

2 hospital
visit
wrote

3 sir

To Be Great

historical fiction by Eileen M. Berry
illustrated by Alfredo Belli

1 ## The Letter

President Lincoln sat at his desk thinking. He had a pile of mail in front of him. Many of the letters, like the one at the top of the stack, were about the war.

America had split into two sides. Both sides were fighting with each other, and many men had been killed. People were praying that the war would end. President Lincoln felt sad as he sat thinking.

The top letter on his stack was from his friend. His friend's son, Jed, was in the war. Jed was just sixteen, but he had done a bad thing. He had run away from a battle. Soldiers who ran from battles were punished. Jed's father asked President Lincoln to forgive his son and keep him from being punished.

President Lincoln wanted to do what was
right. Jed had run from the battle, but he was
just a teen.

The president had sons of his own. He was
thinking of what they would have done.

Just then the president's son Tad peeked in.
"Pa," he said, "is it time to play yet?"
President Lincoln gazed at Tad and did not
say anything.
"Pa?" said Tad.
"We will play in a little while, Tad."

2 The Deal

The president picked up his pen.
"I will make a deal with Jed," he said. "I will forgive him, but he must go back to the battle. He must stay till the war is done. He must not run from a battle ever again."

The president wrote a letter to Jed's leader.
Then he put his name in big letters: *A. Lincoln*.

Tad peeked in again. "Pa," he said, "is it time
to play?"
President Lincoln smiled at Tad. "Yes, Tad," he
said. "What game will we play?"
"We can play leapfrog!" Tad squealed.

The president set his pen on his desk and went
to play with Tad.

For many weeks the war went on. One day President Lincoln put on his hat. He said, "I will be back. I need to go to the city hospital to visit the men who got shot in the war."
"May I come with you, Pa?" asked Tad. "Please?"

The president stopped at the door. "It will not be
fun, Tad," he said. "Many men are bleeding from
gunshots. You will see men who are very sick."

"Please let me come, Pa," said Tad.

"Well," the president thought, "maybe the
men would like to see Tad. Maybe he can
make them smile."
He smiled at Tad. "You may come," he said.
"But you must not run and play at the hospital.
You must keep still and stay with me."
"I will," said Tad.

3 The Visit

At the hospital, the men were on the cots in rows. President Lincoln went from cot to cot. He held one man's hand. He spoke to another man quietly. He smiled into each face.

Tad stayed close to his father and kept still.

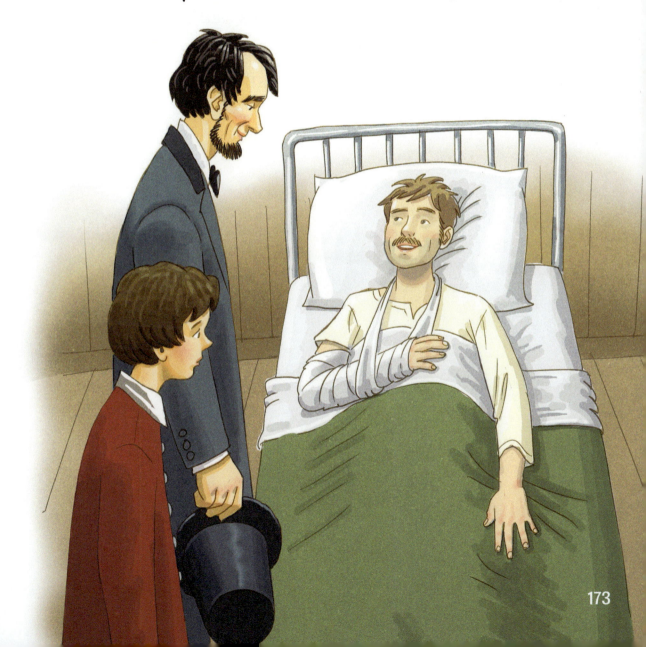

One soldier sat up when the president came to his cot. "Mr. President," he said.

"Yes?" President Lincoln smiled at him.

"My name is Jed. My father is your friend. He sent you a letter asking you to forgive me. If it were not for you, sir, I would have been punished weeks ago. I ran from a battle, but you forgave me. I went back to the fighting, sir, just like you said. I want to thank you, sir."

The president nodded. "It is I who must thank you. Thank you for fighting for us. What happened to you in the battle?"

"I got shot in my leg, sir. I was afraid, but I did not run."

The president gripped Jed's hand. "A brave soldier may be afraid, but he does not run."

"Is this your son, Mr. Lincoln?" asked Jed.
"Yes, this is Tad," said the president. Tad
smiled at Jed.

Jed smiled back. "Pleased to meet you, Tad,"
he said. "It was nice of you to come. Your
father is a great man. You would do well to
be like him some day."

President Lincoln spoke to his son. "Tad, it is a great thing to be president. And it is a great thing to be brave. Jed is a brave lad. You would do well to be like him."

"Thank you, sir." Jed's eyes were wet when the president and Tad left.

After Reading

1. Why does a man write a letter to President Lincoln?
2. What does Tad want to do with his father?
3. Who does President Lincoln say that Tad should be like?

Think & Discuss

Have you ever had to try again after you failed at something?
Did it take courage to try again?

"In God have I put my trust:
I will not be afraid."
Psalm 56:11

Understanding New Words

How can you understand a word you do not know? You can look at the other words in the sentence. You can look at the illustrations. After you read the whole sentence and look at the illustrations, read the sentence again. Did you figure out the meaning of the new word?

Can you find these words in the story? What do you think they mean?

succulent collide
ravine   abyss

Learning to Ski with Mr. Magee

fantasy written and
illustrated by Chris Van Dusen

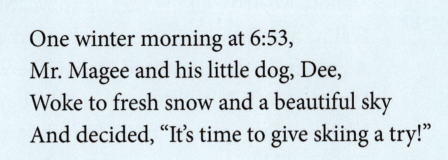

One winter morning at 6:53,
Mr. Magee and his little dog, Dee,
Woke to fresh snow and a beautiful sky
And decided, "It's time to give skiing a try!"

"Before we drive all the way up to Mt. Snow,
Follow me, Dee, I know right where to go.
Across from the house and just up the way
Is a great little hill with a view of the bay.
We'll practice up there 'til we learn how to ski,
Then we'll head for the mountain," said
Mr. Magee.

A few minutes later they came to a spot
Where nothing could get in their way,
Magee thought.
So he put on his skis. Dee hopped in the pack.
And with poles in his hands and his dog on
his back,
He inched to the edge very slowly until his
skis teeter-tottered, then started downhill!

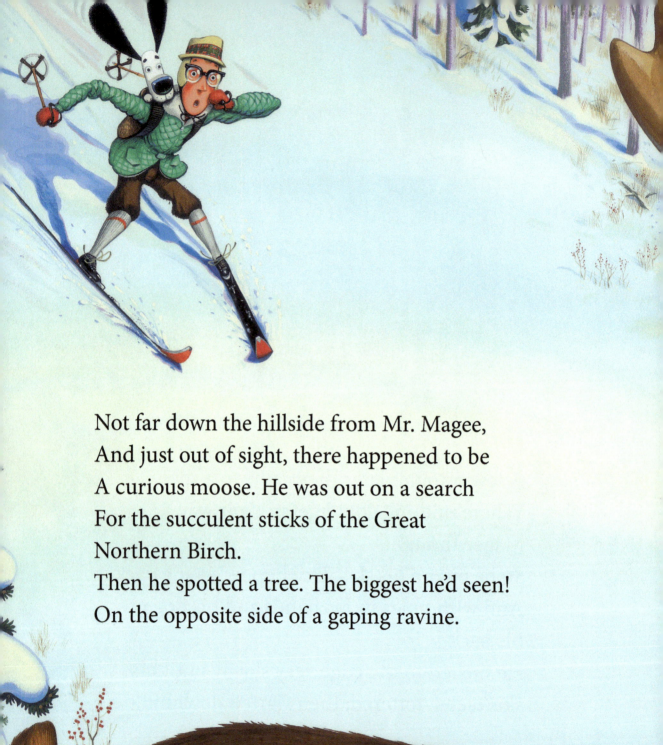

Not far down the hillside from Mr. Magee,
And just out of sight, there happened to be
A curious moose. He was out on a search
For the succulent sticks of the Great
Northern Birch.
Then he spotted a tree. The biggest he'd seen!
On the opposite side of a gaping ravine.

The moose turned around and what did he see?
Mr. Magee and his little dog, Dee!
The moose was so shocked he stood frozen in fear.
But Mr. Magee hadn't learned how to steer!
And he knew very soon they were going to collide,
So he called to the moose, "Would you please
step aside?!"

But the moose didn't move. So Magee yelled,
"DUCK!"
And that was the moment they ran out of luck.
'Cause while they were sliding right under
the moose,
The tips of the skis snagged the log of a spruce!

In a flash and a flip they flew over the log,
Tossing poor Mr. Magee and his dog
Head over heels straight into the gap . . .

When the ends of the skis came down with a slap!
So there they were stranded, Magee and his pup,
Across a ravine, a hundred feet up!

They hung there, suspended, not making a sound.
When the moose came back, he looked all around.
He didn't see Dee or Magee—but what's this?
A bridge to the birch above the abyss!

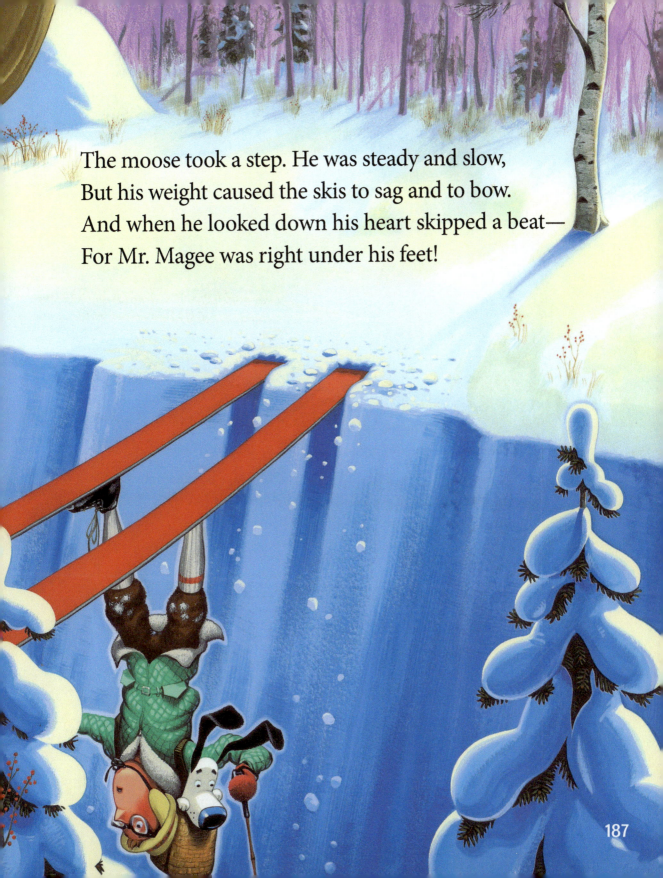

The moose took a step. He was steady and slow,
But his weight caused the skis to sag and to bow.
And when he looked down his heart skipped a beat—
For Mr. Magee was right under his feet!

187

With a snort the moose leapt!
The skis went SPRING!

188

They popped in the air with a ZIP and a ZING!
And up like a rocket shot Dee and Magee,

Landing feet first just as
safe as can be!

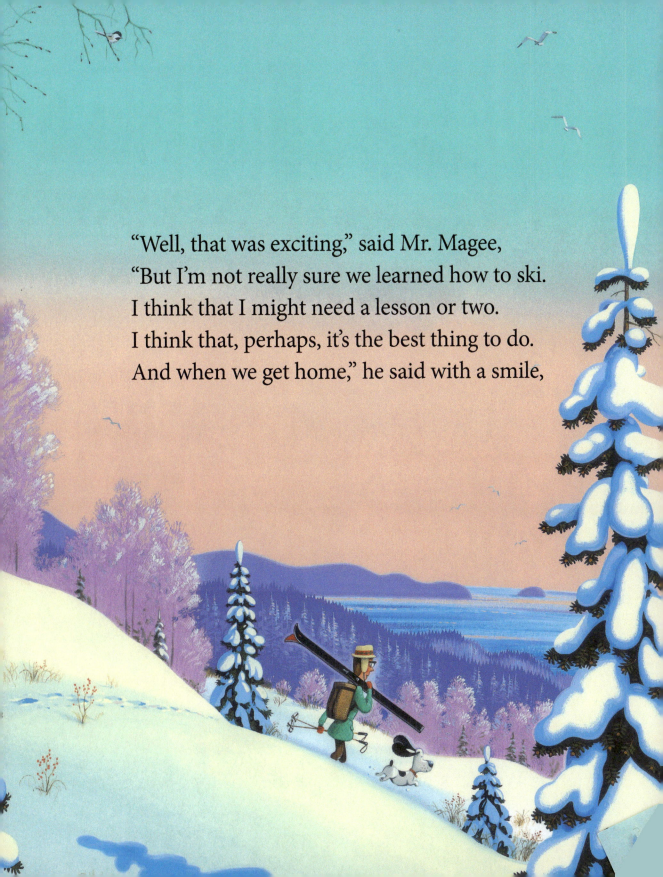

"Well, that was exciting," said Mr. Magee,
"But I'm not really sure we learned how to ski.
I think that I might need a lesson or two.
I think that, perhaps, it's the best thing to do.
And when we get home," he said with a smile,

"We'll let someone else use the skis for a while."

1. What does Mr. Magee want to learn?
2. What does Mr. Magee almost collide with?
3. What does the moose walk on to cross the ravine?

Think & Discuss

Do you think taking skiing lessons would help Mr. Magee be brave? Why or why not?

Meet the Author and Illustrator

Chris Van Dusen has loved to draw since he was a child. His favorite things to draw were robots and aliens. Now he writes and illustrates stories for children. He also illustrates children's stories by other authors. He lives in Maine with his wife, Lori, and his dog, Opal.

Glossary

A glossary is a list of important or special words and their meanings. A glossary is found at the end of some books. Unlike a dictionary, a glossary contains only words that are used in the book.

This Glossary has information about selected words in this reading book. It gives the meanings of words that are used in some of the selections.

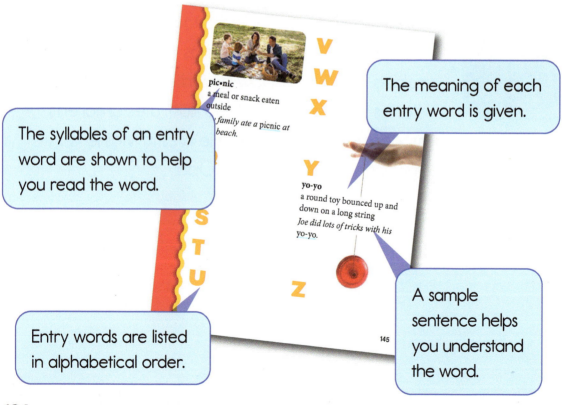

The syllables of an entry word are shown to help you read the word.

Entry words are listed in alphabetical order.

The meaning of each entry word is given.

A sample sentence helps you understand the word.

194

A

a•fraid

fearful, scared

Susie is afraid *of her uncle's big dog.*

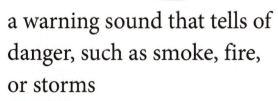

a•larm

a warning sound that tells of danger, such as smoke, fire, or storms

The loud noise of the smoke alarm *woke me up.*

arrow

a sharp pointed stick shot from a bow

King David shot an arrow *from his bow.*

B

bar•ber

someone who cuts hair and trims beards

Dan and his dad went to the barber *for haircuts this morning.*

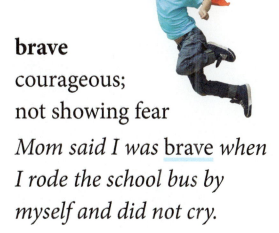

brave

courageous; not showing fear

Mom said I was brave *when I rode the school bus by myself and did not cry.*

C

cab•in

a small, basic house; the place where campers sleep at summer camps

Tim and Tom stayed in the Black Bear cabin *at Camp Hilltop.*

chief

the head or leader of a group

Kate's dad is the fire chief *in her town.*

D

des•ert

a place with hardly any people, very little water, and very few plants

A desert *is usually very hot during the day.*

dough

a soft mixture of flour and other ingredients with liquid; often used to bake bread or cookies

Sarah and her mom baked the bread dough *into pizza crust.*

drag•on

a make-believe monster that looks like a lizard with wings and claws and that sometimes breathes out fire

Cal read a story about a dragon *that lived in a cave.*

flute

a musical instrument shaped like a tube with holes along the side; played by blowing across a hole near one end

Emma played her flute *in the school program.*

frost•ing

a sweet topping for cakes and other desserts

Chocolate frosting *is my favorite part of a cupcake.*

G

H

hear•ing aids

small devices worn in or on the ears to help people hear better

My cousin has worn hearing aids *since he was a baby.*

hy•drant

a pipe next to the street with a nozzle to attach a hose; used to get water from the main pipes under the street

The firefighter attached the hose to the hydrant *and sprayed water on the house fire.*

I

I•raq

an Arab country in the Middle East

My friend Zia's grandpa came to the United States from Iraq.

J

K

L

M

ma•jor

an officer in the military

Nick's dad is a major *in the army.*

milk•man

a man who sells milk or delivers it to customers

The milkman *drives a big truck filled with bottles of milk.*

N

O

or•na•ments

decorations

Leah and Paul hung ornaments *on the Christmas tree.*

P

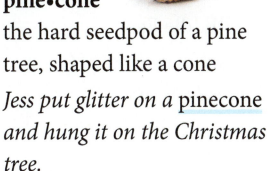

pine•cone

the hard seedpod of a pine tree, shaped like a cone

Jess put glitter on a pinecone *and hung it on the Christmas tree.*

pro•tect

to keep safe; to guard

A loving father will protect *his children.*

si•ren

a device that makes a loud sound as a warning

I heard the siren *as the police car came down the street.*

Q

Iran

Iraq

Saudi Arabia

Qa•tar

a small Arab country in the Middle East

The small country of Qatar *is mostly desert.*

sol•diers

members of an army

The soldiers *worked to protect the people.*

sta•tion

a place or building where a person usually stands or where a certain job is done

The students went to the fire station *on a class trip.*

sun•set

the time when the sun goes down; evening

We walked on the beach and watched the sunset.

sun•rise

the time when the sun starts to come up; early morning

Silas and his dad got up at sunrise *to go fishing.*

T

tad•poles

newly hatched frogs or toads

Titus looked for tadpoles *in the lake.*

U

U•nit•ed States

a large country in North America that includes fifty states

Alaska is part of the United States.

V

W

wade

to walk through water

Ana took off her shoes to wade *in the rain puddles.*

wor•ship

to love and honor God

The Bible says to worship *only the one true God.*

yule

Christmas

Sophia loves to decorate for the yule season.

Photo Credits

Key: (t) top; (c) center; (b) bottom; (l) left; (r) right; (bg) background; (i) inset

Glossary

Text Acknowledgments

Unit 3